THE ULTIMATE
JAMES
HORNER
FILM SCORE COLLECTION

Wise Publications
part of The Music Sales Group
London/New York/Paris/Sydney/Copenhagen/Berlin/Madrid/Hong Kong/Tokyo

Published by
Wise Publications
14-15 Berners Street, London W1T 3LJ, UK.

Exclusive Distributors:
Music Sales Limited
Distribution Centre, Newmarket Road,
Bury St Edmunds, Suffolk IP33 3YB, UK.
Music Sales Pty Limited
4th floor, Lisgar House, 30-32 Carrington Street,
Sydney, NSW 2000, Australia.

Order No. AM1011109
ISBN: 978-1-785580826
This book © Copyright 2015 Wise Publications,
a division of Music Sales Limited.

Compiled and edited by Jenni Norey.
New arrangements by Vasco Hexel.
Music processed by Paul Ewers Music Design.
Cover designed by Tim Field.
Photographs courtesy of Picture-desk.com - The Kobal Collection.
Background images by Les Cunliffe - Fotolia.
Printed in the EU.

The Amazing Spider-Man
(Promises/End Titles)
7

An American Tail
(Somewhere Out There)
12

Apollo 13
(The Launch)
26

Avatar
(I See You)
18

A Beautiful Mind
(All Love Can Be)
29

Braveheart
(For The Love Of A Princess)
34

Deep Impact
(The Wedding)
42

Legends Of The Fall
(The Ludlows)
37

The Mask Of Zorro
(Zorro's Theme)
50

The Perfect Storm
(There's No Goodbye Only Love)
46

Star Trek II: The Wrath Of Khan
(Theme)
53

Titanic
(My Heart Will Go On)
58

Introduction

When James Horner died in an aviation accident in June of 2015,
Hollywood lost one of its most prolific and popular composers.
That popularity was never in doubt, even if the sheer scale of Horner's
output came as a surprise to many when the films he had scored
were assembled into a formidable list.

If many knew him as the composer of 'My Heart Will Go On'
thanks to Céline Dion and *Titanic* (1997), fewer were aware that
he had been producing film scores since 1979 when his film career
was launched with *The Lady In Red*, a depression-era gangster movie
that prompted producer Roger Corman to hire Horner to score his remake
of *Seven Samurai* set in space, *Battle Beyond The Stars* (1980).

For classically-trained James Horner, working for Corman was
a colourful start, although his breakthrough was to come two years later
scoring *Star Trek II: The Wrath of Khan*. After that the big films just
kept coming his way for over 30 years, earning him two Academy Awards,
two Golden Globe Awards, three Satellite Awards, three Saturn Awards
and three BAFTA nominations.

As this superb collection demonstrates James Horner could seemingly
rise to any challenge: superhero blockbuster, children's animated feature,
period drama, true-life space epic and emotional disaster movie.
These twelve pieces are perhaps the cream of a very rich crop.

THE AMAZING SPIDER-MAN
Promises/End Titles

Music by James Horner

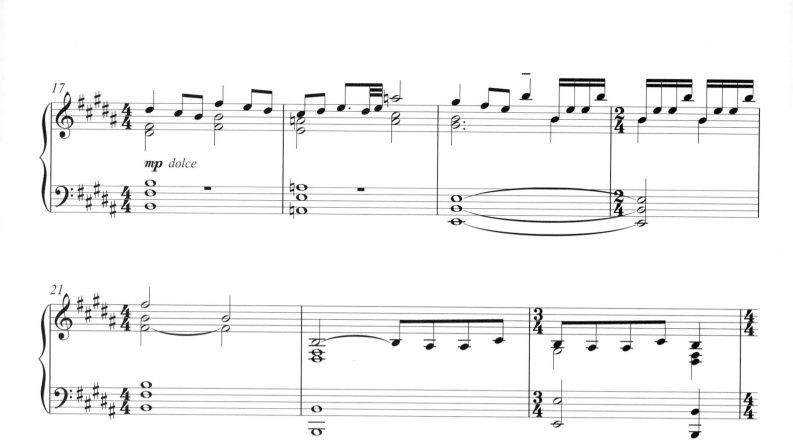

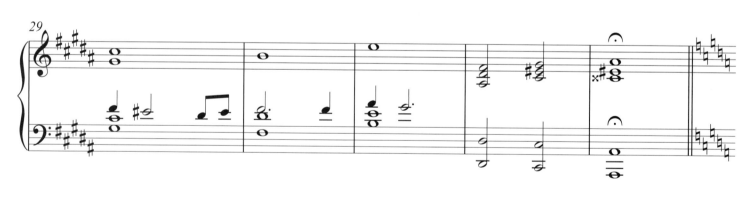

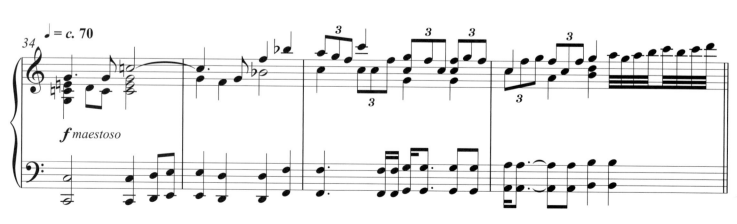

9

10

AN AMERICAN TAIL
Somewhere Out There

Words & Music by James Horner, Barry Mann
& Cynthia Weil

27 **Fmaj7**   **G/F**   **F**   **G/F**

helps to think_ we might_ be wish - in' on the same_ bright_ star. And

29 **A♭**   **B♭/A♭**   **A♭**   **B♭/A♭**

when the night_ wind starts to sing a lone - some lul - la - by it

poco rit.   **a tempo**

31 **A♭**   **B♭/A♭**   **G**

helps to think we're sleep - ing un - der - neath the same big sky.

34 **C**   **Em7**   **Fmaj9**   **F/G**   **C**   **C/E**   **F**

Some - where out there if love can see us through,

then we'll be to - geth - - er some-where out there, out where dreams come

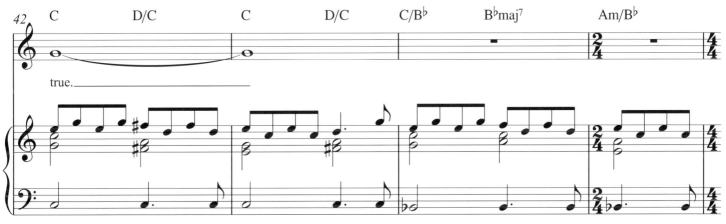

true._____

15

helps to think we're sleep-ing un-der - neath the same big sky.

Some-where out there if love can see us though,

then we'll be to-geth - er some-where out there, out where dreams come

true.

AVATAR
I See You

Words & Music by James Horner, Simon Franglen
& Thaddis Harrell

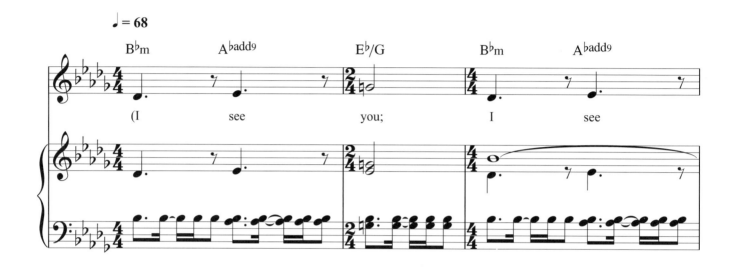

en - chant-ing.__ I pray in my heart that this dream nev - er ends.__

I see me through your eyes,_____

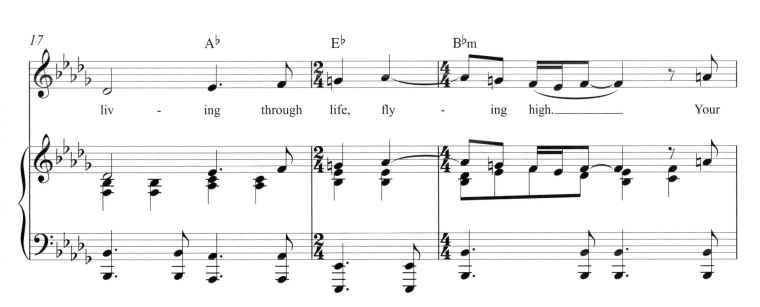

liv - ing through life, fly - ing high._____ Your

19

love shines the way in-to pa - ra-dise, so I of - fer my life as a

sac - ri - fice. I live through your love._____ 2. You

teach me how to see all that's__ beau-ti - ful._____ My sen - ses touch your world I've nev - er

21

22

to the world that you have shown me,

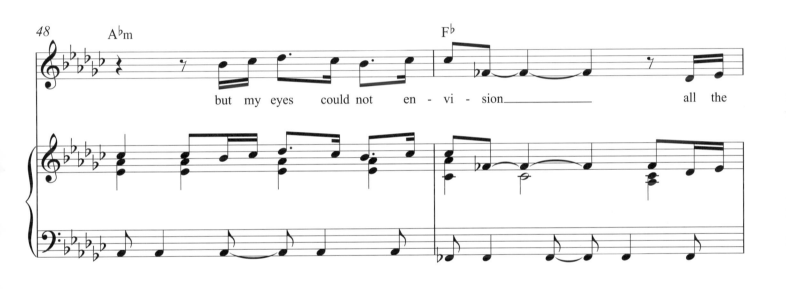

but my eyes could not en - vi - sion all the

col - ours of love and of life ev - er more, ev - er

23

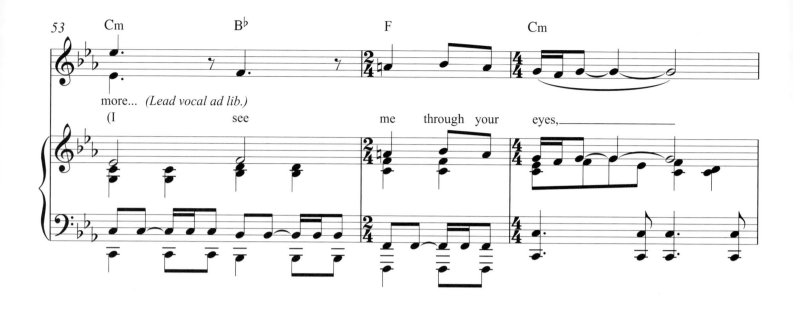

more... *(Lead vocal ad lib.)*
(I see me through your eyes,_____

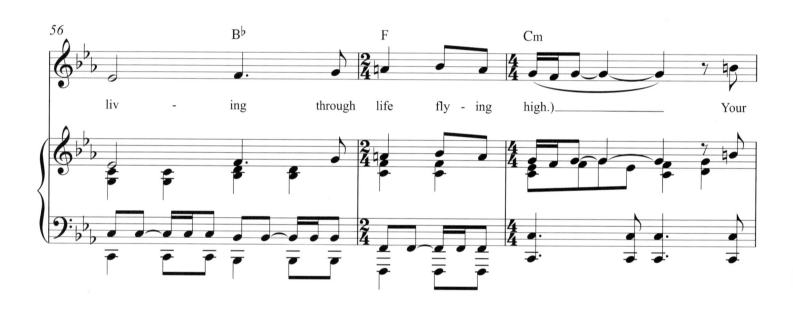

liv - ing through life fly - ing high.)_____ Your

love shines the way in - to pa - ra - dise, so I of - fer my life as a

APOLLO 13
The Launch

Music by James Horner

A BEAUTIFUL MIND
All Love Can Be

Words by Will Jennings
Music by James Horner

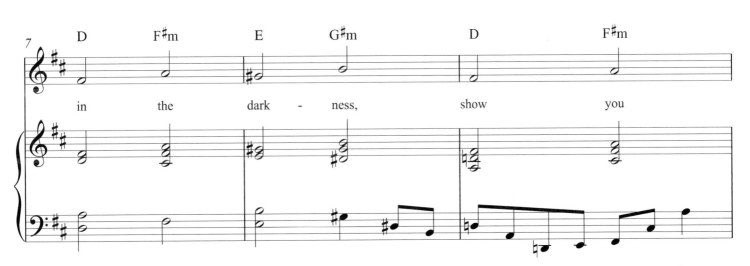

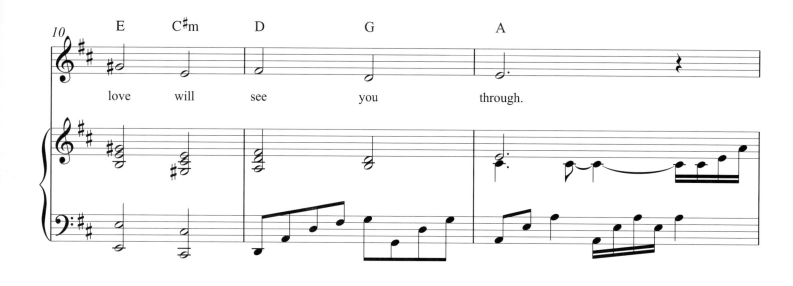

love will see you through.

When the bad dreams wake you

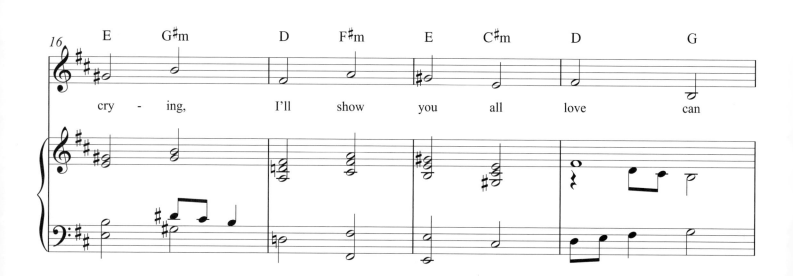

cry - ing, I'll show you all love can

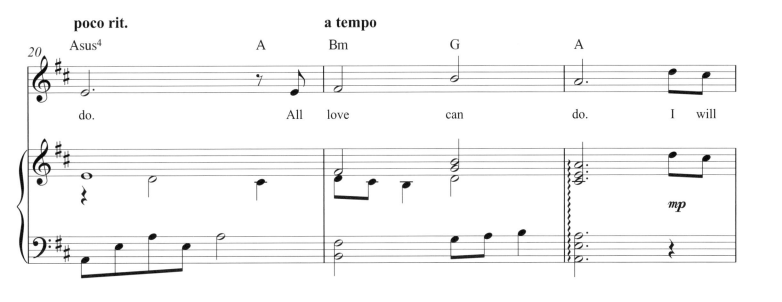

31

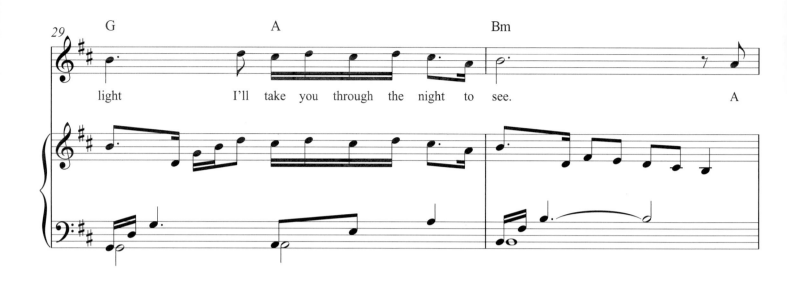

light   I'll take you through the night to see.   A

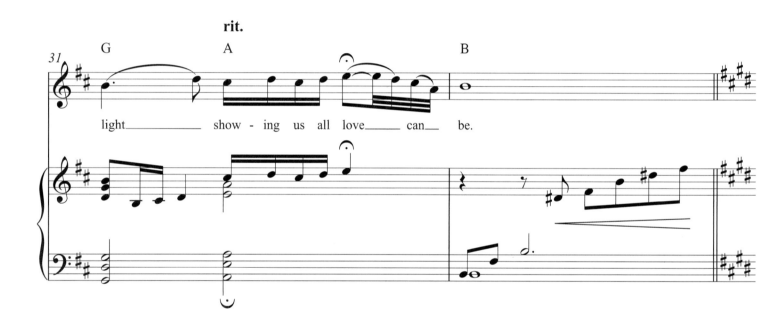

light_____ show - ing us all love____ can__ be.

I   will   guard   you   with   my

bright   wings.   Stay   till   your   heart   learns   to

see.   All   love___   can   be.

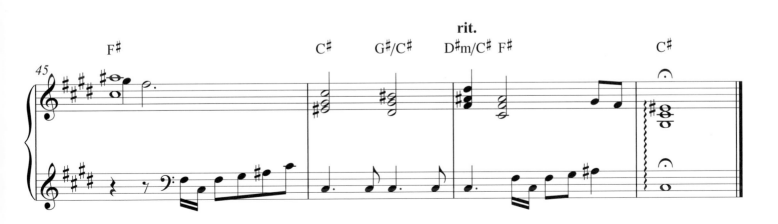

BRAVEHEART
For The Love Of A Princess

Music by James Horner

LEGENDS OF THE FALL
The Ludlows

Music by James Horner

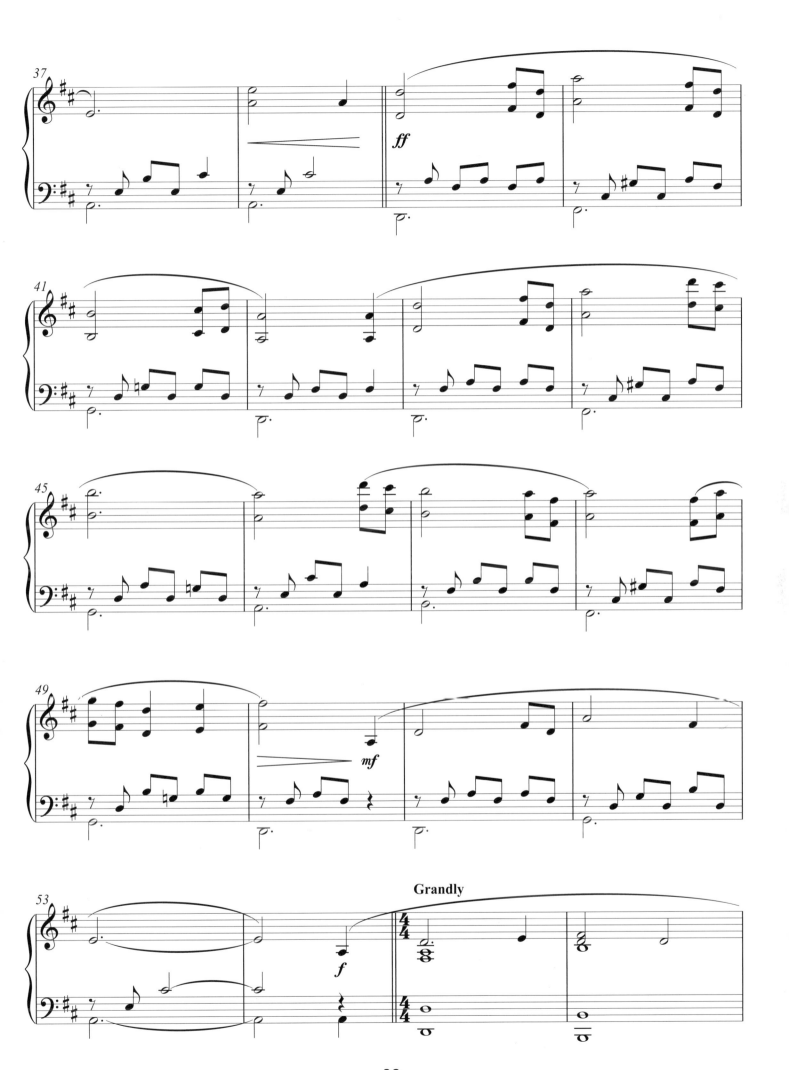

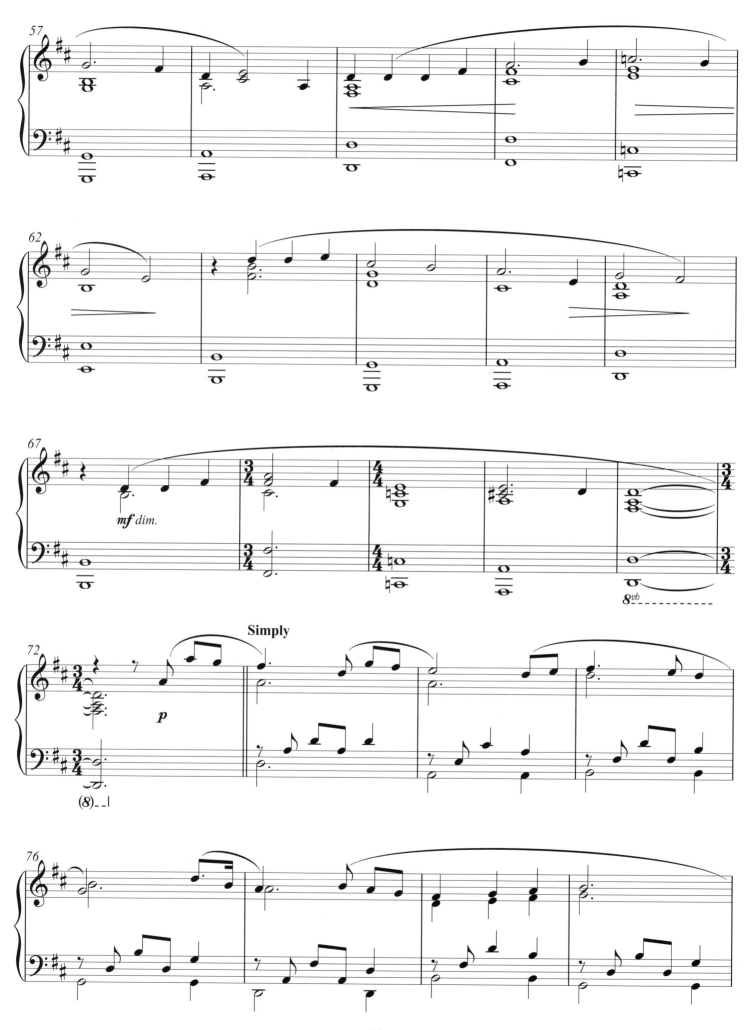

40

DEEP IMPACT
The Wedding

Words & Music by James Horner

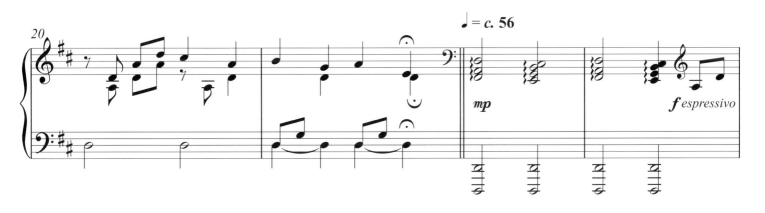

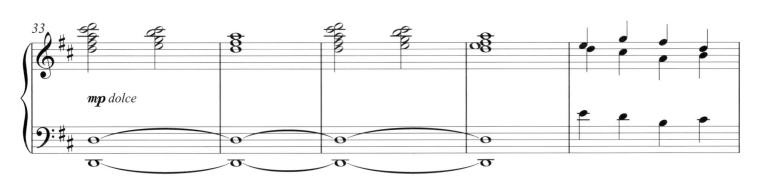

44

THE PERFECT STORM
There's No Goodbye Only Love

Music by James Horner

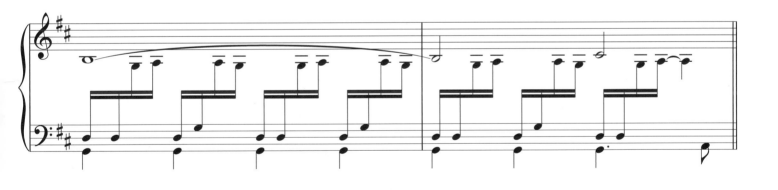

48

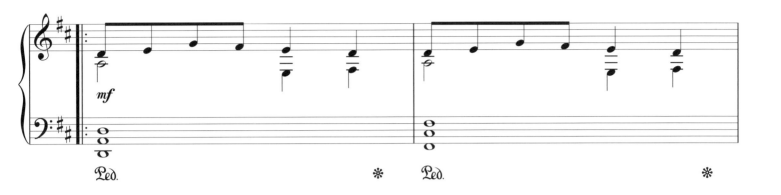

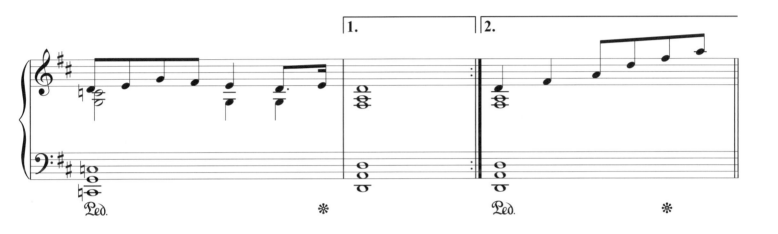

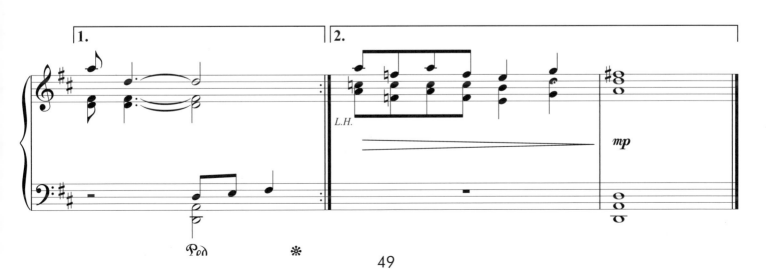

THE MASK OF ZORRO
Zorro's Theme

Music by James Horner

52

STAR TREK II: THE WRATH OF KHAN
Main Theme

Music by James Horner

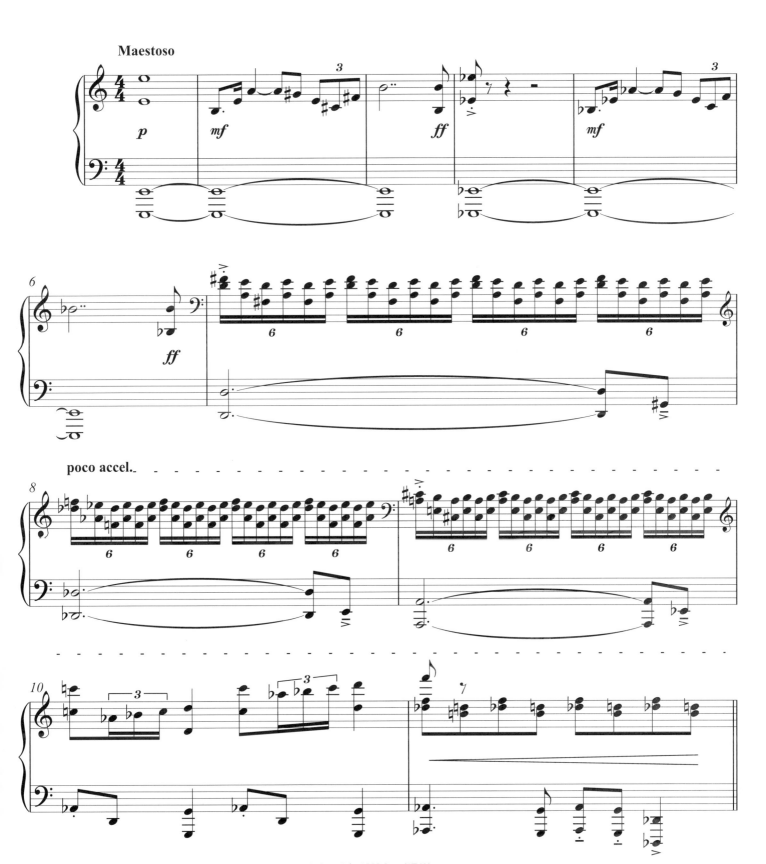

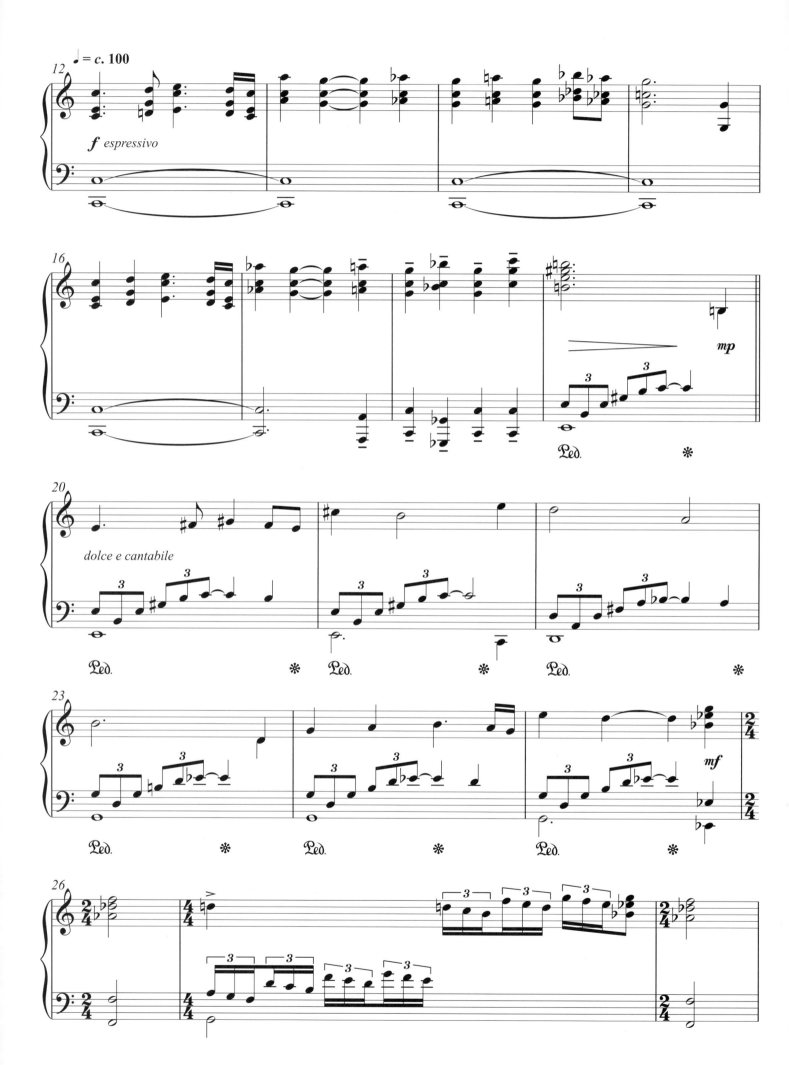

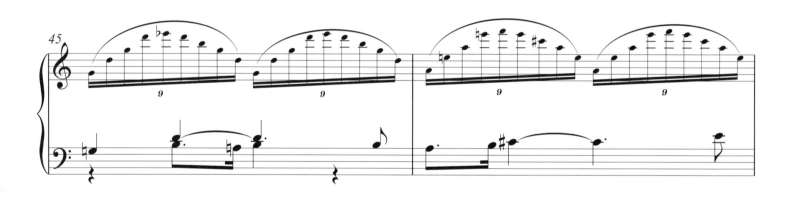

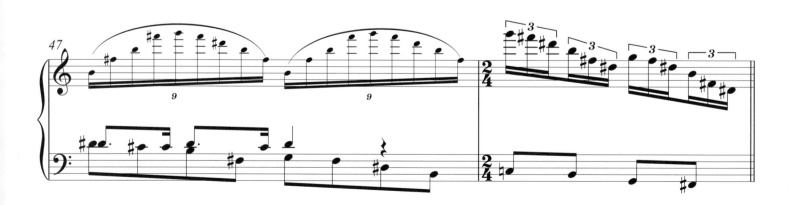

TITANIC
My Heart Will Go On

Words by Will Jennings
Music by James Horner

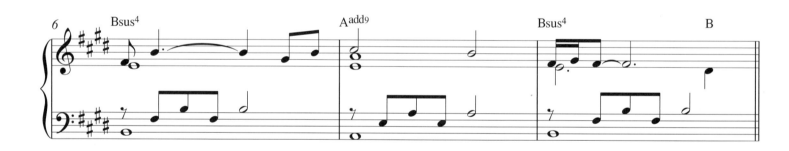

1. Ev - 'ry night in my dreams I see you, I
2. Love can touch us one time and last for a

Con pedale

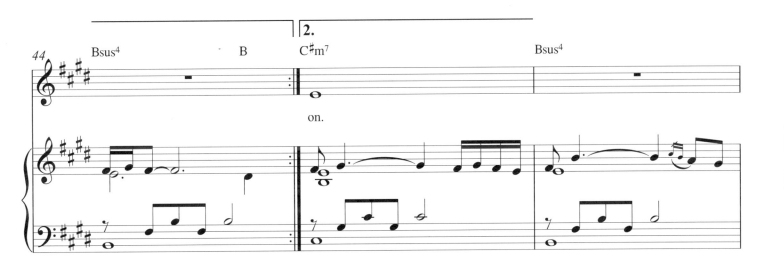

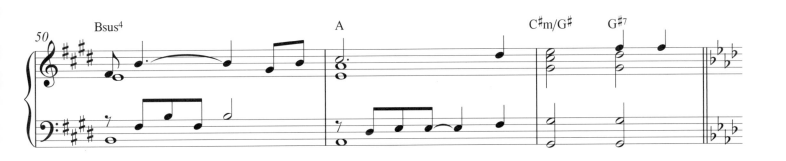

Whatever you want...

Music Sales publishes the very best in printed music for rock & pop, film music, jazz, blues, country and classical as well as songs from all the great stage musicals.

Many of our practical publications come with helpful CDs or exclusive download links to music files for backing tracks and other audio extras.

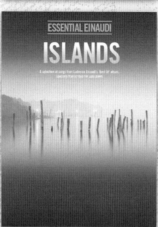

We also publish a range of tuition titles, books for audition use and book+DVD master classes that let you learn from the world's greatest performers.

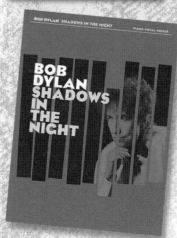

So, whatever you want, Music Sales has it.

Just visit your local music shop and ask to see our huge range of music in print.

In case of difficulty, contact marketing@musicsales.co.u